French Fashion Designers

BRIGIT VINEY

Level 2

Series Editors: Andy Hopkins and Jocelyn Potter

Pearson Education Limited
Edinburgh Gate, Harlow,
Essex CM20 2JE, England
and Associated Companies throughout the world.

ISBN 0 582 435633

First published 2001

Text copyright © Brigit Viney 2001
Illustration for "Words in Fashion" by Richard Gray

Design by Neil Alexander
Colour reproduction by Spectrum Colour
Printed and bound in Denmark by Norhaven A/S, Viborg

Published by Pearson Education Limited in association with Penguin Books Ltd,
both companies being subsidiaries of Pearson Plc

Photograph acknowledgements:
Daniel Simon/Gamma: p. 3; Corbis: p. 5; Rex Features: pp. 6, 7, 11, 13, 16, 17, 20, and 21;
Popperfoto: pp. 9, 14, and 15; Erik Russel/Everyday Pictures: pp. 24 and 25.

contents

Introduction

France was and is a center of fashion.

Who made France a center of fashion? And who makes it a center now? This book tells you about the many famous designers of French fashion—men and women, young and old. What are they famous for? How did they start to work in fashion? Read about their interesting lives and their important designs.

French fashion designers changed women's clothes in many ways between 1900 and 2000. Women do more now—at work, at home, and in sports—and they have the right clothes for their lives. They wear pants, not long dresses, and T-shirts, not corsets. French designers were important in these changes in fashion.

The world of fashion is always interesting. The clothes are often beautiful or strange, and always very expensive. They are from a different world. What happens in this world? Who designs for the big fashion houses? How do designers make their designs? What happens before a fashion show? This book tells you about the work of a fashion house. It also gives you an idea of the business of French fashion and its place in France and Europe.

Maybe the clothes in this book will give you ideas for designs. Can *you* be a designer? Answer the questions on page 19 and see!

Brigit Viney follows fashion from her home. She likes wearing T-shirts, pants, and sports shoes.

What do you know about French fashion designers?

Answer these questions.

1 Which of these designers was not born in France?
a Jean-Paul Gaultier   **b** Sonia Rykiel   **c** Yves Saint Laurent

2 Which of these names is only a company, not a person?
a Agnès B   **b** Chloé   **c** Lacroix

3 What was "Coco" Chanel's first name?
a Catherine   **b** Gabrielle   **c** Jeanne

4 Who designed the "New Look" of 1947?
a Christian Dior   **b** Hubert de Givenchy   **c** Jean Patou

5 Who was famous for the "little black dress"?
a Christian Dior   **b** Chanel   **c** Nina Ricci

6 Who has the Rive Gauche stores?
a Chanel   **b** Christian Dior   **c** Yves Saint Laurent

7 Who designed a skirt for men in 1985?
a Jean-Paul Gaultier   **b** Claude Montana   **c** Emanuel Ungaro

8 Who made "Mondrian" dresses in 1965?
a André Courrèges   **b** Pierre Cardin   **c** Yves Saint Laurent

9 What colors does Christian Lacroix like?
a dark colors   **b** light colors   **c** strong colors

10 Who makes the "Kelly bag"?
a Balmain   **b** Hermès   **c** Louis Vuitton

Answers
1. c   2. b   3. b   4. a   5. b   6. c   7. a   8. c   9. c   10. b

Words in fashion

stockings

tie

cardigan

sweater

corset

suit

jewelry

blouse

scarf

boots

suit

perfume

make-up

Clothes from a fashion house

Fashion houses are famous for their haute couture clothes. These clothes are very expensive because the fashion house makes them by hand for a very small number of customers. Often the fashion house makes only about six of each dress or skirt. It makes them the right size for each customer. Each dress costs maybe $30,000–$45,000. Only about two or three thousand people in the world buy these clothes.

Ready-to-wear clothes from designers are in their stores. They have the designer's name on them. They are expensive: jeans from Chloé cost about $375. Some designers also make clothes for the woman—or man—in the street. These clothes are much cheaper.

Designers show their haute couture clothes in January and July. They show clothes in January for the spring/summer, and they show clothes in July for the fall/winter. Ready-to-wear shows are in February/March for the fall/ winter, and in September/October for the spring/summer. Fashion houses can pay $750,000 or more for a ready-to-wear show. Ready-to-wear shows are the most important because they are in newspapers around the world.

A Chanel haute couture suit

3

Chanel

Chanel is an old and famous French fashion house. "Coco" Chanel opened it in 1915.

Gabrielle ("Coco") Chanel was born in 1883 in the French town of Saumur. Her life was difficult. Her parents did not have much money for their five children. When her mother died, her father sent Gabrielle and her sisters to a school for girls. She never saw her father again.

When she left school, Gabrielle sang in bars. Here she got her name "Coco" and met Etienne Balsan, a rich young man. He took her to his large house in the country and Chanel began to make simple hats for his friends. In about 1909 she moved to Paris and started to sell hats. A year later she opened a hat store with help from her new rich English lover, Arthur ("Boy") Capel. In 1913 she opened a clothes store, again with help from Boy Capel. The store was in the famous vacation town of Deauville. In it Chanel sold women's clothes for sport and the beach. She made a lot of them from jersey. (Before this, jersey was a material for men's sports clothes and underclothes.) Women could move easily in these jersey clothes and they did not have to wear corsets with them. They enjoyed this.

In 1915 (in the First World War) Chanel opened a store and a fashion house in Biarritz. She sold a lot of clothes and she was famous in Europe and the United States. She opened more workrooms in Paris after the war.

In 1921 she began to sell her perfume, Chanel No.*5. Its simple name and bottle were very different from other perfumes. It was the first perfume with a designer's name. Chanel lived on the money from it for fifty years.

Chanel liked using men's clothes for women. She put men's sweaters with skirts, and made wide pants for women.

*No.: short for "number"

Coco Chanel in a jersey suit.

She dressed women in jersey suits, raincoats, shirts, cardigans, and big jackets. In 1926 she started to design her famous "little black dresses." They were simple and very beautiful. With them women wore Chanel jewelry.

Chanel loved jewelry, and her lovers gave her a lot of it. She did not wear it often because she did not want to look very rich. In the 1920s she began the fashion for artificial jewelry. She designed and sold large, colorful jewelry. It went well with her simple clothes.

In 1936 nearly 4,000 people worked for Chanel and she sold nearly 28,000 designs each year. But when the Second World War (1939–45) started, Chanel stopped making clothes. She had a Nazi* lover and in 1944 she had to leave France.

*Nazi: a follower of Adolf Hitler

She went to Switzerland and did not go back to France for ten years.

When she opened her fashion house in Paris again, she showed jersey suits and dresses. The French did not like them because they were not fashionable. But Americans bought them, and after three years Chanel was an important designer again. Everybody wanted a Chanel suit.

In the 1950s and 1960s many things were "Chanel": her suits, her white blouses, her bags, her light brown-and-black shoes, her jewelry. This was the Chanel "look."

Chanel died in 1971. For the next twelve years the House of Chanel did not do very well. Then in 1983 the designer Karl Lagerfeld started to work for them. Lagerfeld uses ideas from Chanel and also from the streets of London and New York. Young people like his clothes because his ideas are new, smart, and sometimes funny.

Karl Lagerfeld's ideas are new and smart.

Christian Dior

In the Second World War, and after it, women in Europe and the United States wore shorter skirts. Material was expensive, so people did not use much of it. Then in February 1947 the designer Christian Dior showed some very different clothes. His skirts were longer and very wide. They used a lot of expensive material—sometimes fifty meters for a dress. The American newspapers called his designs the "New Look." A lot of women wanted this look because it was pretty and different from wartime fashion. Dior was suddenly famous, and Paris, not London or New York, was the center of haute couture again.

Dior was forty-two, and this was his first collection. His work in fashion began in 1935, at the age of thirty. He sold designs to fashion houses and magazines. He worked for the designers Piguet and Lelong, and then in 1946 he started a small fashion house with money from a very rich man, Marcel Boussac. Dior began with three workrooms and eighty-five workers. He wanted to make very good, very expensive clothes.

The "New Look" was

Dior's "New Look"

not really new. Dior used designs from the 1900s and gave them a look for the 1940s. Women had to wear corsets under these clothes, but in them they felt beautiful. After the difficult years of the war this was wonderful.

Some people did not like his clothes because they used a lot of material. Food and houses were more important than expensive clothes. Chanel did not like his clothes because women could not move in them easily. This was not important to Dior. He only wanted to make beautiful clothes.

In his next collection the skirts were bigger and longer. In 1948 the other Paris fashion houses showed "New Look" designs. Other companies made cheaper "New Look" clothes and women everywhere bought them.

Between 1947 and 1957 Dior designed thirty new collections. In some years he designed four new collections, in other years two. There was the H line of fall 1954 and there were the A and Y lines of 1955. For ten years, Dior made fashion. Everybody waited for his next collection.

From the beginning, Americans were very important customers for Dior because they had more money than the Europeans. In 1948 he called his first perfume "Miss Dior" because he wanted to sell it to Americans.

Dior's couture house got bigger very quickly. In the 1950s he had twenty-eight workrooms and more than 1,000 workers in Paris. Twenty-five thousand customers visited the Paris house each year. The company also got much bigger. There was a Dior house in London and there were stores in North and South America. Dior sold ready-to-wear clothes and gave his name to shoes, bags, jewelry, scarves, stockings, and ties. Dior Perfumes began to sell make-up. The name Dior was everywhere and the company made a lot of money. Haute couture was now big business.

In 1957 Dior died suddenly after only ten years in his haute couture company. The young Yves Saint Laurent was

John Galliano designs very beautiful and exciting clothes.

the new designer. He had some good new ideas but he left in 1960. Then Marc Bohan came to Dior and went back to Dior's lines. But now, in the 1960s and 1970s, other designers had more interesting and exciting ideas. They were more important in haute couture than Dior.

In 1997 the 35-year-old British designer John Galliano came to Dior. Galliano has many unusual ideas and he designs very beautiful and exciting clothes. He is making Dior an interesting fashion house again.

Yves Saint Laurent

After Christian Dior died in October 1957, the head designer at Dior was the 21-year-old Yves Saint Laurent. He was a quiet, intelligent young man from Oran, Algeria. Christian Dior met him when he was a student in Paris. His designs were wonderful, so Dior gave him a job. He began to work for Dior in 1955. At the time it was the most famous fashion house in the world.

In January 1958 Saint Laurent showed his first collection at Dior. Everybody loved it and he was in the newspapers. Dior's customers liked his next collections but they hated his fall/winter collection for 1960. In this he used ideas from the clothes of young people in the street. He designed a lot of black clothes—black suits, jackets, and coats. Dior's older customers did not want them.

In 1961 Saint Laurent and his lover, Pierre Bergé, started a new couture house. The first collection was in January 1962. It was good, but his second collection was wonderful. In it he used a simple long jacket. Workmen usually wore these jackets, but he used them in couture. (Chanel did the same in the 1920s.)

His other collections in the 1960s had a lot of beautiful clothes and new ideas. In 1963 he showed very long boots; in 1965 he made "Mondrian" dresses. Most buyers of haute couture were older people, but these first collections were for young people. But later Saint Laurent's designs changed and were for older people. In 1966 he made the famous "smoking" suit for women. *Le smoking* is the French name for men's jackets for dinner parties.

The pant suit of 1969 was a famous design. For Saint Laurent it was his most important design because it gave men's clothes to women. Pants were the YSL look. Women began to wear them to work.

Saint Laurent could always see and understand the ideas of the time. In the 1960s young people did not want beautiful designer clothes. These clothes were from their parents' way of life. Saint Laurent understood this.

In the next thirty years Saint Laurent had many more ideas and was the most important designer of his time. For many people his 1976 "Russian" collection was his best collection, with its long, wide skirts, boots, and scarves. For him, his best collections were from 1980 and 1988. These used ideas from Picasso and Braque.

In 1966 Saint Laurent and Bergé opened the first Rive Gauche store in Paris. This was the first ready-to-wear store by a haute couture house. In the 1960s and 1970s they began to sell other things: perfume, men's clothes, and make-up. These made a lot of money.

One of Yves Saint Laurent's best collections—from 1988.

After about 1978 Saint Laurent did not go to many parties. He did not want to meet people. These days he goes to his haute couture shows, but that is all. He does not talk to the newspapers very often.

In 1993 Saint Laurent and Bergé sold the ready-to-wear and perfume businesses to Sanofi. In 1999 Sanofi sold them to Gucci. The haute couture is a different company. Saint Laurent designs two collections for it every year. He is in his sixties, but he does not want to stop working. He loves his work and his fashion house.

Jean-Paul Gaultier

Jean-Paul Gaultier was born in Paris in 1952. When he was fourteen he began to design clothes. He did not go to school very often because he wanted to learn about make-up and hair from his grandmother. At seventeen he sent some ideas to some important designers and in 1970 Pierre Cardin gave him a job for a year. Cardin was famous for his men's suits and his unusual ideas for women's clothes. Cardin liked using new materials, and Gaultier liked them too.

In 1971 Gaultier worked for Jacques Esterel, and then for Jean Patou. In 1974 he worked for Cardin again—this time in the Philippines. There he designed collections for the United States. In 1976 he showed his first ready-to-wear collection in Paris. He made some dresses from wallpaper and other unusual things. The fashion buyers did not understand his ideas. For a time, the Paris fashion world did not think well of him and he could not find money in France for his company. Then in 1978 the Japanese company Kashiyama gave him money. Three years later he got money from two Italian companies.

Gaultier's ideas in the 1980s came from the street fashion in London. People wore short hair in different colors, black make-up, and strange jewelry. Gaultier used things from the kitchen for jewelry, and used clothes in unusual ways. Jeans were stockings, and corsets were evening clothes. Sometimes his friends or people from the street wore his clothes in the fashion shows. He was the "bad boy" of fashion. He liked this.

In 1985 he showed his "skirt" for men. He also showed men in sweaters without backs, little hats, and other women's clothes. This was very unusual in the West because men did not wear women's clothes. Why not? People began to think.

Madonna liked his designs, and in 1990 Gaultier designed some clothes for her. He made her a corset and a man's dark

Jean-Paul Gaultier's skirt for men.

suit. It was a famous look, maybe because it used men's and women's clothes.

In 1999 the old company Hermès bought 35% of Gaultier's haute couture, ready-to-wear, and perfume business. This was good for Gaultier because now he had the money of a large company. Hermès wants to open Gaultier stores in different countries. Gaultier's name is also good for Hermès because he is new and famous.

Gaultier's clothes are funny, smart, and beautiful. He can put men into short skirts, but he can also make beautiful evening dresses for women. He enjoys life; his designs show that.

A love of color
and new ideas

Emanuel Ungaro

Emanuel Ungaro is a lover of color. He was born in 1933 in Aix-en-Provence, in France, to Italian parents. His father made clothes for men, and Ungaro worked with him. Then in

1955 he went to Paris and worked in a small company. They made men's clothes too. Later he worked with Balenciaga and André Courrèges. But in 1965 Courrèges sold his business to L'Oréal. Then Ungaro opened a fashion house in his very small apartment in Paris.

Ungaro's first designs for his company were very short skirts and long boots—clothes for "the future." Now he uses a lot of very strong colors and flowery materials.

Emanuel Ungaro uses a lot of flowery materials.

Christian Lacroix

In 1987 a new haute couture house opened in Paris. It was the first new house for nearly twenty years. Its designer was 36-year-old Christian Lacroix. The money for the company came from Bernard Arnault. Arnault is now the head of the very large company LVMH (Louis Vuitton Moët Hennessy). LVMH has Lacroix and also Christian Dior, Givenchy, Céline, and Kenzo.

Lacroix is famous for his strong colors, beautiful materials, and pretty skirts and dresses. He gets many ideas for his designs from very old clothes. Often his ideas are unfashionable, but he does not want to follow fashion.

Lacroix also likes designing for the theater. He says, "My work for the theater and my work for couture are very close."

Christian Lacroix is famous for his strong colors.

Thierry Mugler

Thierry Mugler is very different from Ungaro and Lacroix. His clothes are very unusual. They are clothes for the future too. In them women and men are ready for anything.

Mugler was born in Strasbourg in 1948. In 1968 he went

to Paris and worked in a fashion store. Two years later he began to sell designs to different fashion houses, and in 1973 he designed his first collection: "Café de Paris." In this he had a little black suit, a raincoat, and a small hat: clothes of the 1940s, not of the 1970s. Later the city suit was Mugler's look, but it was a city suit of the theater, not the office. In 1977 he

Thierry Mugler's clothes are very unusual.

showed his collection in a new way. It was theater—not a fashion show. Now other designers show their collections in this way too.

Claude Montana

Claude Montana (1949–) likes unusual clothes too. He works very well in leather. In his big jackets and coats of the 1970s people looked strong and angry. Montana uses strong colors: black, red, and gray. He is not afraid of ugly clothes.

Julien Macdonald

One day, Karl Lagerfeld saw some beautiful and unusual sweaters in England. Who was the designer? A smart young man from Wales—Julien Macdonald. Lagerfeld loved Macdonald's designs. The two men talked about fashion and later Macdonald worked with Lagerfeld.

Claude Montana works very well in leather.

   Today Macdonald is the head designer at Givenchy. He was only 28 years old when Givenchy gave him the job. Macdonald has a lot of famous friends—models, designers, and singers. He makes very expensive and very small dresses for some of his friends—but he is famous for his beautiful sweaters.

Work in a
fashion house

A designer starts work on his or her new ready-to-wear collection after the show of the old collection. Sometimes the designer starts work on the day of the show.

Ready-to-wear shows happen six months before the clothes go into the stores. So designers start work on the new collection twelve months before the clothes go into the stores. They make sixty or seventy designs for each collection.

Designers have to think about the future. What will people want to wear next year? What is changing? They have to get ideas for the future from the world now. What is happening in movies, music, and television? What are people wearing in the street? They also have to think about last year. What clothes did people like? What did we sell?

The designers talk about their ideas with their design assistants and start to buy materials. They draw their designs and send them to the pattern cutters. These people make the patterns from the designs. They have to understand the designer's drawings, and the materials. Then other people in the workrooms make the clothes and show them to the designer. The designer, design assistants, and pattern cutters look at the clothes and change them. When everybody is happy with the design, people can start to make the clothes for the show. (For haute couture, they do this by hand.)

Hat, shoe, and jewelry designers also make designs for the show. The designer puts the hats, shoes, and jewelry with the clothes. The show designer makes the show from the different designs.

After the show, clothes buyers buy the clothes for their stores. And it all starts again.

Can you be a
fashion designer?

Answer these questions.

1 Do you like clothes and fashion?
   a Yes, very much. **b** Yes, a little. **c** No, not much.

2 Are you interested in the world?
   a Yes, a little. **b** No, not much. **c** Yes, very much.

3 Do you change your clothes into more interesting clothes?
   a Yes, always. **b** Yes, sometimes. **c** No, never.

4 Do people say that your clothes are unusual?
   a Sometimes. **b** All the time. **c** Never.

5 When do you think of the color of your clothes?
   a Sometimes. **b** When I put them on. **c** Not often.

6 Do you make your clothes?
   a Yes, all of them. **b** Yes, some of them. **c** No, I can't.

7 Can you draw?
   a Not very well. **b** Yes, I'm not bad. **c** Yes, very well.

8 Do you follow fashion?
   a Yes, I always buy fashionable clothes.
   b No, I'm not interested in it. **c** No, I start fashions.

Women designers

Sonia Rykiel

Sonia Rykiel (1930—) began to design clothes in 1962. She wanted to wear good clothes before she had her baby. She could not find any, so she made some. Her friends liked them, so she began to sell them in her husband's stores. She opened her first store in Paris in May 1968.

Rykiel did not want to follow fashion, so her clothes were

very different. She made—and makes—a lot of sweaters and cardigans, long skirts, wide pants, and easy jackets. They are often light brown, gray, dark blue, and black. (She only wears black.) She often uses jersey. Her designs are not always fashionable, but they are always strong.

Sonia Rykiel's designs are always strong.

Martine Sitbon

Martine Sitbon was born in 1951 in Morocco to a French father and an Italian mother. She moved to Paris when she was ten. After she studied at a design school in Paris, she went to Hong Kong, Mexico, and India. She was away for seven years. In 1985 she showed her first collection, and from 1987 to 1991 she was the designer for the ready-to-wear company Chloé.

Sitbon's designs use many different materials. Sometimes she uses them in unusual ways. She can make a man's shirt in a very thin material, or a man's hat in a very beautiful material. She does not usually use strong colors.

A Martine Sitbon design for Chloé.

Agnès B

Agnès B (Agnès Troublé) started work in 1958 with *Elle* magazine at the age of seventeen. Two years later she began to design for the stores Dorothée Bis. In 1964 she left them and designed clothes for different companies. In 1975 she opened a store in Paris. Women of all ages liked her clothes. They were fashionable but also simple. She uses simple materials and colors (often black). Her clothes are for all women—not only very rich women.

Lolita Lempicka

Josiane Pividal was born in 1954 in Bordeaux. Her mother made pants at home and Pividal learned from her. In 1983 she started a fashion company with her husband. They called it "Lolita Lempicka." When their company was famous, they changed their names to Lolita and Joseph-Marie Lempicka. This was easier because usually fashion houses have the names of their designers. Lempicka/Pividal is famous for her beautiful suits.

Isabel Marant and Catherine Malandrino

Isabel Marant and Catherine Malandrino are two younger designers. Marant makes clothes for young women between fifteen and thirty-five. She likes using ideas from Africa and India. Malandrino works in New York. She uses hot, strong colors and beautiful materials. She is famous for her American hats in different colors.

Cristina Ortiz and Stella McCartney

Many of the women in French fashion are not French. There is Cristina Ortiz, the Spanish designer at Lanvin. And there is Stella McCartney, the British designer. She was at Chloé before she moved to Gucci. McCartney, the daughter of Paul and Linda McCartney, went to Chloé as head designer in 1997. She was twenty-five. Her most famous designs are her jeans and her short dresses.

The business
of fashion

France was and is a center of fashion. But does fashion make money for France?

France sells its fashion to other countries, but it sells many other products too. In 1995 only 2% of the money from other countries came from clothes. (In Italy it was 6%.) Another 2% came from perfume and make-up. In France the number of workers in fashion (clothes, perfume, jewelry, shoes) is small—about 206,000. This is about 0.9% of the French workers in France. There are only about 6,000 people in haute couture.

France does not sell the most fashion. Italy and Germany sell more than France. But France sells more of the very expensive fashion products than other countries, and it is important in the perfume and make-up businesses. French companies make 25% of all perfume and make-up from Europe.

Haute couture companies sell a lot of clothes to other countries, and 65% of their money comes from these clothes. Perfume companies make 41% of their money in the same way.

Most of the haute couture companies do not now only sell clothes to a small number of women. They want to sell a lot of ready-to-wear clothes, perfume, and jewelry, so they want unusual clothes in their shows. Photos of these clothes go into the newspapers.

Most French fashion houses want to sell to young people. The old fashion houses want young designers because they will bring new ideas. So Dior has John Galliano and Givenchy has Julien Macdonald.

Bags, jewelry, perfume

Fashion is not only about clothes. It is also about bags, shoes, scarves, and jewelry. The company Hermès is famous for beautiful headscarves and for the Kelly bag. They made the Kelly bag in 1935. Grace Kelly often carried one, so in 1955 Hermès gave it her name. A lot of people buy it today. Louis Vuitton is also famous for its bags. The company makes them from unusual and expensive leathers. But Hermès and Louis Vuitton now also

A Hermès Scarf

make ready-to-wear clothes. The Belgian Martin Margiela designs for Hermès, and the American designer Marc Jacobs works for Louis Vuitton.

The big fashion houses also sell bags and many other products: scarves, ties, jewelry, shoes, boots, sports shoes, sunglasses, watches, make-up, perfume. Perfume is a very important money-maker for fashion houses. It brings some houses about 80% of their money.

A Louis Vuitton bag

The first designer's perfume was Rosine. Paul Poiret made it in 1911 and called it after his daughter. Then Coco Chanel made Chanel No. 5 in 1921 and Jeanne Lanvin made Arpège in 1927.

Sunglasses by Chloé

The most expensive perfume is Joy by Jean Patou. Patou started selling it in 1926. It used a very large number of flowers. Other designers—Dior, Givenchy, Ricci—followed in the 1940s and 1950s. L'Air du Temps by Ricci and Chanel No. 5 sold very well in the 1960s and 1970s. (Marilyn Monroe was a famous wearer of Chanel No. 5.) Younger designers make perfumes too: Jean-Paul Gaultier, Sonia Rykiel, Agnès B.

Designer products are not cheap: a Kelly bag costs about $3,300. Dior sunglasses cost $220 and a Hermès watch costs about $900. But people pay a lot of money for a designer's name.

Perfume by Dior

Who are you?

Answer these questions.

1 You are at a party. What are you wearing?
   a jeans and a T-shirt
   b a long dress with a corset/pants and a shirt
   c a dark suit with a white blouse/with a shirt and tie

2 You are going to a friend's house in the country for lunch. It is winter. What will you wear?
   a a warm coat, a warm sweater, jeans, and thick shoes
   b a leather jacket and boots
   c a raincoat and thin shoes

3 Tomorrow is your first day at work in a busy office. What will you wear?
   a jeans and a white shirt
   b pants, a T-shirt, and a lot of jewelry
   c a suit with a blouse/with a shirt and tie

4 You are going with some friends to the beach for the weekend. Which three things will you take?
   a a T-shirt, jeans, sunglasses
   b a little black dress, your Chanel bag, some perfume/your best black T-shirt, your best jeans, your Dior sunglasses
   c a suit, a scarf, your computer

5 You are going to a football game. What will you wear?
   a a T-shirt and jeans
   b your best T-shirt, a leather jacket, and a short leather skirt/some pants
   c an expensive shirt and pants

Now look at page 28 for the answers.

ACTIVITIES

Pages 1–13

Before you read

1 Discuss these questions. Find the words in *italics* in your dictionary.

    a Are you interested in *fashion*? Are your clothes *fashionable*?

    b Which French *designers* do you like? What do they *design*?

    c Do you like *haute couture* clothes? Do you have any?

    d Which *material* do you like best? Why?

2 These words have different meanings in fashion. What are they? Look in your dictionary and then find the meaning below.

  a *collection* a *line* a *look* *ready-to-wear* a *show*

    a Beautiful women wear a designer's new clothes. People take photos of them and write about them.

    b Your clothes, shoes, hair, and bags make this.

    c These designer clothes are in the stores.

    d A number of new clothes from a designer.

    e Clothes make this on a person. An A- . . . . . dress makes an "A."

3 Find these words in your dictionary. Put them in the sentences.

  artificial *business* *jersey* *simple* *unusual* *war*

    a The fashion . . . . . makes a lot of money.

    b Because this design is . . . . . you can make it easily.

    c In a . . . . . ., people want food, not fashion.

    d "Is this flower really a flower?" "No, it's . . . . . . "

    e This perfume is very different. It's very . . . . . .

    f I like . . . . . dresses because I can move in them easily.

After you read

4 Are these sentences right or wrong?

    a Chanel used corsets very often in her designs.

    b Dior only worked in his fashion house for ten years.

    c Yves Saint Laurent is famous for his pant suits.

    d Gaultier now works for Hermès.

5 "Fashion designers only design for rich, thin women." Talk about this with other students.

Pages 14–26

Before you read

6 Find the words below in your dictionary. Which word is:
a a material? **b** a person? **c** a picture?
assistant   drawing   leather   pattern   product
What are the other words in your language?

After you read

7 Answer the questions.
a Who gets many ideas from old clothes?
b When do ready-to-wear shows happen?
c Which country sells the most fashion?
d Why do many fashion houses sell perfume?

8 Work with another student.
Student A:
You are an important fashion designer. Ask Student B
questions about his/her ideas.
Student B:
You are a young designer and you want to work with Student A.
Talk to him/her and ask for a job.

Writing

9 Write about a designer's show for a fashion magazine.
10 You are a fashion designer. Write about two of your designs
and draw them. Where did your ideas come from?
11 You are Chanel. What do you think of fashion today? Write a
letter to a friend.
12 Your fashion house has a new perfume. Write about it for a
magazine. What is its name? Who will buy it? Why?

Answers to page 26

Most of your answers were "a":
You like the simple life! But don't be boring! Try different, more interesting clothes for work and parties.
Most of your answers were "b":
You're a party girl/boy! But sometimes simple clothes are better for vacation or the office.
Most of your answers were "c":
You're a hard worker! But don't forget—there's life outside the office.